Letts
gets you through

C000156322

KS2 ENGLISH
SATs SUCCESS
PRACTICE TEST PAPERS

Ages 10–11

KS2
ENGLISH
SATs

4 complete tests

PRACTICE
TEST
PAPERS

SHELLEY WELSH AND
LAURA GRIFFITHS

Contents

(pull-out section at the back of the book)

ACKNOWLEDGEMENTS

The authors and publisher are grateful to the copyright holders for permission to use quoted materials and images.

p 81–83 Extract from *Street Child* by Berlie Doherty, published by HarperCollins Publishers. Reprinted by permission of David Higham Associates Ltd.
p 86–88 Extract from *James and the Giant Peach* by Roald Dahl, published by Penguin Books Ltd. Reprinted by permission of David Higham Associates Ltd.
p 91–92 *Macavity*, from *Old Possum's Book of Practical Cats* by T.S. Eliot. Reprinted by permission of Faber and Faber Ltd.

p 87 © LiliGraphie/Shutterstock.com.
p 89 © ALAMY p 90 © ALAMY
All other images are © Shutterstock.com

Every effort has been made to trace copyright holders and obtain their permission for the use of copyright material. The authors and publisher will gladly receive information enabling them to rectify any error or omission in subsequent editions. All facts are correct at time of going to press.

Published by Letts Educational
An imprint of HarperCollins*Publishers* Ltd
1 London Bridge Street
London SE1 9GF

ISBN: 978-0-00-830053-1

First published 2018

10 9 8 7 6 5 4 3 2

Text, Design and illustration © Letts Educational, an imprint of HarperCollins*Publishers* Ltd 2018

British Library Cataloguing in Publication Data.

A CIP record of the book is available from the British Library.

Series Concept and Development: Michelle l'Anson
Commissioning Editor: Alison James
Authors: Shelley Welsh and Laura Griffiths
Editorial: Jill Laidlaw and Richard Toms
Cover Design: Amparo Barrera and Paul Oates
Inside Concept Design: Ian Wrigley
Text Design and Layout: Aptara®. Inc.
Artwork: Letts Educational, Aptara®. Inc. and Jouve India Private Limited
Production: Lyndsey Rogers
Printed by CPI Group (UK) Ltd, Croydon, CR0 4YY

Introduction and instructions

Key Stage 2 SATs and how these practice test papers will help your child

The KS2 SATs are taken at the end of Year 6 (age 11). Here's a breakdown of the tests:

Maths	English reading	English grammar, punctuation and spelling
Paper 1: arithmetic (30 minutes)	Reading (1 hour)	Paper 1: questions (45 minutes)
Paper 2: reasoning (40 minutes)		Paper 2: spelling (approximately 15 minutes)
Paper 3: reasoning (40 minutes)		

This book is made up of two sets of English practice test papers. Each set contains similar test papers to those that your child will take at the end of Year 6 in English reading and English grammar, punctuation and spelling. They can be used any time throughout the year to provide practice for the Key Stage 2 tests.

The results of both sets of papers will give a good idea of your child's strengths and weaknesses.

Administering the tests

- Provide your child with a quiet environment where they can complete each test undisturbed.
- Provide your child with a pen or pencil, ruler and eraser.
- The amount of time given for each test varies, so remind your child at the start of each one how long they have and give them access to a clock or watch.
- You should only read the instructions out to your child, not the actual questions (unless instructed otherwise).
- Although handwriting is not assessed, remind your child that their answers should be clear.

English reading

- Each test is made up of three different texts and an answer booklet.
- Answers are worth 1, 2 or 3 marks, with a total number of 50 marks for each test.
- Your child will have **one hour** to read the texts in the reading booklet and answer questions in the answer booklet.
- Some questions are multiple choice, some are short answers where only a word or phrase is required, and others are longer with several lines to write the answer.
- Encourage your child to look at the mark scheme after each question to help them know how much detail is required in their answer.

English grammar, punctuation and spelling

Paper 1: questions
- Each answer is worth 1 mark, with a total of 50 marks available.
- Your child will have **45 minutes** to complete the test paper.
- There are different types of questions in this paper. The space given shows the type of answer that is needed.

Paper 2: spelling
- Contains 20 spellings, with each spelling worth 1 mark.
- Your child will have approximately **15 minutes** to complete the test paper.
- Using the spelling test administration guide on pages 101–102, read each spelling and allow your child time to fill it in on their spelling paper.

Marking the practice test papers

The answers and mark scheme have been provided to enable you to check how your child has performed. Fill in the marks that your child achieved for each part of the tests.

Please note: these tests are **only a guide** to the standard or mark your child can achieve and cannot guarantee the same is achieved during the Key Stage 2 tests, as the mark needed to achieve the expected standard varies from year to year.

English reading

	Set A	Set B
English reading paper	/ 50	/ 50

The scores achieved on these practice test papers will help to show if your child is working at the expected standard in English reading: 13–25 = working towards the expected standard; 26–38 = working at the expected standard; 39–50 = working above the expected standard.

English grammar, punctuation and spelling

	Set A	Set B
Paper 1: questions	/ 50	/ 50
Paper 2: spelling	/ 20	/ 20
Total	/ 70	/ 70

The scores achieved on these practice test papers will help to show if your child is working at the expected standard in English grammar, punctuation and spelling: 20–35 = working towards the expected standard; 36–52 = working at the expected standard; 53–70 = working above the expected standard.

When an area of weakness has been identified, it is useful to go over these and similar types of questions with your child. Sometimes your child will be familiar with the subject matter but might not understand what the question is asking. This will become apparent when talking to your child.

Shared marking and target setting

Engaging your child in the marking process will help them to develop a greater understanding of the tests and, more importantly, provide them with some ownership of their learning. They will be able to see more clearly how and why certain areas have been identified for them to target for improvement.

Top tips for your child

Don't make silly mistakes. Make sure you emphasise to your child the importance of reading the question. Easy marks can be picked up by just doing as the question asks.

Make answers clearly legible. If your child has made a mistake, encourage them to put a cross through it and write the correct answer clearly next to it. Try to encourage your child to use an eraser as little as possible.

Don't panic! These practice test papers, and indeed the Key Stage 2 tests, are meant to provide a guide to the standard a child has attained. They are not the be-all and end-all, as children are assessed regularly throughout the school year. Explain to your child that there is no need to worry if they cannot do a question – tell them to go on to the next question and come back to the problematic question later if they have time.

Key Stage 2

English reading

Reading answer booklet

Time: 21:31

You have **one hour** to read the texts in the reading booklet (pages 75–83) and answer the questions in this answer booklet.

Maximum mark	Actual mark
50	

First name	Jack				
Last name	Gray				
Date of birth	Day	16	Month	May	Year	2012

5

1 Where is the scene set?

In a garden

1 mark

2 Why is Alice very small?

She drunk a magic potion

1 mark

3 Look at the opening conversation.

Find and **copy** the clause Alice says just before she sits down at the table.

what are you talking about
theres plenty of room

1 mark

4 Which character offers Alice a drink?

Tick **one**.

the Hare ☑

the Hatter ☐

the Narrator ☐

the Dormouse ☐

1 mark

5 Why is Alice angry?

the hare said have some wine but there was nothing on the table

6 **Alice:** *Then it wasn't very **civil** of you to offer it!*

What does the word *civil* mean in this line?

Tick **one**.

polite	☐
angry	☑
old	☐
rude	☐

7 Look at the Narrator's opening lines.

Find and **copy** the words that suggest Alice is correct in saying there is room for her to sit down.

all squashed at one end

8 Explain why Alice says, *'it's very rude!'*.

_____

_____
1 mark

9 Towards the end of the passage the Narrator says, *'The conversation drops'*.

What does the word *drops* mean in this context?

_____
1 mark

10 Which adjective best describes Alice during the tea party?

Tick one.

unconfident ☐

impressed ☐

amused ☐

frustrated ☐
1 mark

11 The Narrator refers to the Hatter as 'the Mad Hatter'.

What does the Hatter do that might make him appear 'mad'?

_____

_____
1 mark

12 Look at the title of the extract: *A Mad Tea Party*.

Explain fully why this is an appropriate title, referring to the text in your answer.

_____

_____

_____ 1 mark

13 *The characters continue arguing until the Hatter opens his eyes very wide and begins talking in **riddles**.*

Which word below is closest in meaning to *riddle*?

Tick **one**.

solution ☐

puzzle ☐

sentence ☐

argument ☐ 1 mark

14 Explain the role of the Narrator in the extract.

_____

_____ 1 mark

15 Write **one** word that refers to the mechanism of the Hatter's watch.

_____

1 mark

16 **Hare:** (meekly) It was the *best* butter?

Why is the Hare's response to the Hatter funny?

_____

_____

1 mark

17 What is the name of the largest island of the Isles of Scilly?

_____

1 mark

18 *The Isles of Scilly are made up of five* **inhabited** *and approximately 140 other islands.*

What does the word *inhabited* mean?

Tick **one**.

deserted ☐

far away ☐

people live there ☐

tropical ☐

1 mark

19 Look at the paragraph beginning: *To reach the Isles of Scilly from the mainland . . .*

Give **two** ways visitors can reach the islands.

1. _____

2. _____

1 mark

20 Read the advantages and disadvantages of the two methods of transport.
Which would you recommend for the following visitors?
Give reasons for your answers **using the information in the text.**

A day visitor with no luggage: _____

_____

_____

_____ 1 mark

A family who are staying for a week who want to see dolphins swimming:

_____

_____

_____ 1 mark

21 Why are the Scilly Isles sometimes described as 'a large, natural greenhouse'?

_____

_____ 1 mark

22 Why might the Skybus flight be cancelled?

_____

_____ 1 mark

23 Compare how someone participating in and someone watching a gig race would be involved.

Participating: _____

_____

Watching: _____

_____

24 List **three** activities that the leaflet suggests for tourists to do when visiting the Isles of Scilly.

1. _____

2. _____

3. _____

25 How do the locals usually travel around the islands? Give **two** ways of travelling around the islands.

1. _____

2. _____

26 In what format are you most likely to see this text?

Tick **one**.

a poster ☐

a travel leaflet ☐

a storybook ☐

a school magazine ☐

27 What is the effect of the words underlined in this sentence?

The Isles of Scilly have many historic landmarks <u>waiting to be explored.</u>

_____

_____

1 mark

28 Put a tick in each row to show whether the statements are **true** or **false**.

Statement	True	False
Hugh Town is a big city with a large population.		
The Isles of Scilly are connected by bridges.		
There are many different types of birds on the islands.		
Shops, restaurants, bars and cafés rely on tourism to make money.		

1 mark

29 *The Isles of Scilly have a **unique** climate . . .*

Which word is closest in meaning to *unique*?

Tick one.

strange ☐

special ☐

warm ☐

humid ☐

1 mark

30 *. . . the long, high building with its rows of barred windows.*

What does the word *barred* suggest about the windows?

_____

_____

31 On page 81 Joseph says, *'It's the whole world, this place is.'*?

Tick **three** things that would make the place where they live *'the whole world'* for Jim.

Tick three.

trees	☐
a school	☐
shops	☐
a hospital	☐
a river	☐

1 mark

32 In which season is the extract set? Give **two** pieces of evidence from the text to support your answer.

_____

_____

2 marks

33 Look at the paragraph *It was impossible to tell one day from the next . . .*

How does Jim know that he's been in the workhouse for a year?

Tick **one**.

He looked at his calendar. ☐

He had had another birthday. ☐

There was ice on the pump handle. ☐

He could tell from the changing seasons. ☐

1 mark

34 *It was then that the little secret promise that had nestled inside him began to flutter into life like a wild thing.*

What is '*the little secret promise*' inside Jim?

_____

1 mark

35 *The teacher **hauled** him off his stool . . .*

Which word below is closest in meaning to *hauled*?

Tick **one**.

poked ☐

pushed ☐

persuaded ☐

pulled ☐

1 mark

36 Why does Jim say he doesn't mind when Mr Barrack is beating him?

_____

_____

1 mark

37 Why do you think Mr Barrack winds a handkerchief around Jim's head and ties it under his chin?

_____

_____

1 mark

38 When Mr Barrack had finished beating Jim, _he flung him like a bundle of rags across the desk._

What **two** things does this suggest about Jim?

1. _____

_____

2. _____

_____

2 marks

39 What reasons does Tip give for not going with Jim?

_____

_____

1 mark

40 What do you think Jim is thinking when he reads the words _God is good. God is holy. God is just. God is love._ in the schoolroom?

_____

_____

1 mark

41 Describe the relationship between the two main characters, Jim and Tip, throughout the extract.

Give examples from the text to support your answer.

_____

_____

_____

_____

_____

3 marks

42 Draw a line to match each event below to show the correct order from 1–6, as it appears in the extract.

Mr Sissons asked for big boys to help. ●	● 1
Jim asked Tip to run away with him. ●	● 2
Jim tried to remember what life outside the workhouse was like. ●	● 3
Tip shared his supper with Jim. ●	● 4
Mr Barrack gave Jim a beating. ●	● 5
Jim decided to climb over the wall and escape. ●	● 6

1 mark

43 **Find** and **copy one** word which suggests Mr Barrack was pleased he had caught Jim talking.

Mr Barrack sprang down from his chair, his eyes alight with anger and joy. 'You spoke!' he said to Jim, triumphant. 'It was you.'

_____

1 mark

44 When describing Jim's feelings throughout the extract, the writer has deliberately chosen language that will have an effect on the reader.

Explain the effect of the words used in the sentence below.

Jim's wild thoughts drummed inside him, so loud that he imagined everyone would hear them.

_____

_____

_____

1 mark

SET
A

English
grammar,
punctuation
and spelling

PAPER 1

Key Stage 2

English grammar, punctuation and spelling

Paper 1: questions

Time:

You have **45 minutes** to complete this test paper.

Maximum mark	Actual mark
50	

First name	
Last name	

Date of birth	Day		Month		Year	

1   What is the **word class** of the underlined words in the sentence below?

An elephant charged through the jungle, trampling the trees.

Tick one.

adjectives ☐

determiners ☐

nouns ☐

adverbs ☐

1 mark

2   Tick the word that is closest in meaning to find out.

Tick one.

choose ☐

discover ☐

invite ☐

repeat ☐

1 mark

3   Circle one verb in each underlined pair to complete the sentences using **Standard English**.

We **was / were** going to play outside on our bikes.

I **done / did** well in my maths test this morning.

1 mark

---

4 Which sentence is punctuated correctly?

Tick **one**.

"wait for me!" shouted Orla. ☐

"Wait for me!" shouted Orla. ☐

"Wait for me"! shouted Orla. ☐

"Wait for me," shouted Orla! ☐

1 mark

5 Which **verb form** completes the sentence?

Olivia and Sandip _____ sandcastles at the beach.

Tick **one**.

was building ☐

is building ☐

were building ☐

builded ☐

1 mark

6 Which sentence below is a **command**?

Tick **one**.

We are baking a cake with Mum. ☐

You like chocolate cake, don't you? ☐

Put the flour and butter in the bowl. ☐

How hungry I am! ☐

1 mark

7 Add the missing **full stops** and **capital letters** to the sentence below. The first one has been done for you.

N
ℵottingham is located in the east midlands the river that runs

through nottingham is called the river trent

1 mark

8 Which sentence must **not** end with an **exclamation mark**?

Tick **one**.

It's been a long time since I've seen you, hasn't it ☐

What a shame we can't meet more often ☐

We had such a brilliant time when we last saw each other ☐

Let's not leave it so long next time ☐

1 mark

9 Draw a line to match each **prefix** to the root word to make a new word.

dis		haul
mis		honest
over		understood

1 mark

10 Insert **two apostrophes** in the correct places in the sentence below.

Emmas cat has had five kittens which are black, though

one has white patches around its eyes; their neighbours

dog will now have six cats to chase!

1 mark

11 Use the **co-ordinating conjunctions** in the box to correctly complete the sentence below.
Use each conjunction **once**.

| or but and |

The books _____ DVDs need returning to the library on

Monday _____ Tuesday, _____ remember

it is closed each day for lunch.

1 mark

12 Insert **two dashes** in the correct places in the sentence below.

William Shakespeare a famous author wrote the play 'Macbeth'.

1 mark

13 Underline the **main clause** in the sentence below.

Although she is younger, my sister is much taller than me.

1 mark

14 Tick one box in each row to show if the sentence is in the **present progressive** or the **past progressive**.

Sentence	Present progressive	Past progressive
While the band was playing, Jamie and I were dancing.		
We are reading about the Romans in history.		
The bell is ringing so we must go inside.		

1 mark

15 Choose **one** of the **question tags** below to complete the sentence.

haven't you	haven't we	didn't you

You've been learning about materials in science, _____?

1 mark

16 Tick the sentence that uses a **dash** correctly.

Tick **one**.

We might go to the park – later it just depends on the weather. ☐

We might go to the park later it just depends on – the weather. ☐

We might go to the park later – it just depends on the weather. ☐

We might go to the park later it just – depends on the weather. ☐

1 mark

17 Which sentence uses the underlined word as a **noun**?

Tick **one**.

We volunteered to pick up the plastic bottles on the beach. ☐

The clouds looked dark and menacing as we walked home. ☐

Our classroom light keeps flickering on and off. ☐

Our teacher said she would book a class trip to the theatre. ☐

1 mark

18 Insert a **comma** in the correct place in the sentence below.

Feeling confident the pianist played to a room full of people.

1 mark

19 Circle the **adjective** in the sentence below.

Mum carefully topped the pudding with some whipped cream.

1 mark

20 Explain how the **modal verb** changes the meaning of the second sentence.

1. William is going to wash the car today.

2. William might wash the car today.

_____

_____

_____

1 mark

21 Draw a line to match the words to the correct sentence type.

How blue your eyes are	question
How old are you	statement
The music was very loud	command
Follow me outside, please	exclamation

1 mark

22 Sami wants to know if the tennis match is on TV tonight.

Write the question he could ask to find out.
Remember to punctuate your sentence correctly.

_____

_____

1 mark

23 Underline the **adverbial phrase** in the sentence below.

Later that evening, we said goodbye and began our journey home.

1 mark

24 Add **three commas** in the correct places in the sentence below.

Mangoes kiwis apples pineapples and strawberries are all types

of fruit.

1 mark

25 Complete the sentence below with the **simple past tense** of the
verbs in the boxes.

When the bell _____ , the teacher _____ into

to ring   to come

the room and _____ us to be quiet.

to tell

1 mark

26 Circle the two words that are **synonyms** in the passage below.

As dawn broke, Jake and Ushma strolled along the beach.

Sunrise was always their favourite time of the day on holiday.

1 mark

27 Use the words below to complete the table.

| ancient | new | small | large | wealthy | poor |

	Synonym	**Antonym**
sad	unhappy	happy
rich		
big		
old		

1 mark

28 Insert a pair of **brackets** in the sentence below.

The skateboard park located behind the playground is to be used by children who are over eight.

1 mark

29 Circle the **adverb** in the sentence below.

Tim had worked hard on his spellings so he was disappointed he didn't finish the test.

1 mark

30 Rewrite the sentence below in the **active** voice.

The ancient ruins were visited by the historians.

_____

1 mark

31 What is the **word class** of each underlined word?

I wish <u>they</u> would be quiet now! _____

I'll brush your hair if you brush <u>mine</u>. _____

1 mark

32 Complete the sentence below with a **noun** formed from the verb <u>calculate</u>.

Jana used a _____ to work out the answer.

1 mark

33 Circle the **preposition** in the sentence below.

The girl walked up the stairs.

1 mark

34 Circle the **possessive pronoun** in the sentence below.

I had remembered my homework but Jamal had forgotten his.

1 mark

35 Rewrite the sentence below as **direct speech**.
Remember to punctuate your sentence correctly.

Mum asked if I'd help her in the garden.

_____

_____

1 mark

36 Underline the **relative clause** in the sentence below.

The old lady who was shouting at her neighbour was feeling angry.

1 mark

37 Write a suitable question to match the answer below.
Remember to use the correct punctuation.

Question _____

Answer   He takes the bus.

1 mark

38 Which two sentences contain a **preposition**?

Tick **two**.

The spider crawled up the wall. ☐

My mum doesn't really like spiders. ☐

I put the spider in the garden. ☐

Mum was so pleased she gave me a hug! ☐

1 mark

39 Write a **pronoun** in the space to make the sentence correct.

The boy ran across the playground but _____ was late again.

1 mark

40 Complete the sentence below with a **contraction** that makes sense.

Why _____ you find your homework?

1 mark

41 Rewrite the underlined verbs in the sentence below so that they are in the **past progressive** form.

While I <u>danced</u> on the stage, I could see that my parents <u>clapped</u> loudly.

42 Add **inverted commas** to punctuate the speech below.

What time does the train leave the station? Mary asked the guard.

Three minutes past ten, the guard answered.

43 Which **punctuation mark** should be used in the place indicated by the arrow?

We ran and ran, even though we were out of breath, we simply

couldn't miss that train.

Tick **one**.

full stop ☐

hyphen ☐

semi-colon ☐

comma ☐

44 Rewrite the sentence below so that it starts with a **subordinate clause**. Remember to punctuate your answer correctly.

I read a book while I was waiting to see the doctor.

_____

1 mark

45 Which of the sentences uses **dashes** correctly?

Tick **one**.

The cat – fast asleep – on the rug – was keeping warm by the fire. ☐

The cat – fast asleep on the rug – was keeping warm by the fire. ☐

The cat fast asleep on the rug – was keeping warm – by the fire. ☐

The cat – fast asleep on the rug was keeping – warm by the fire. ☐

1 mark

46 Write a **noun phrase** containing at least three words to complete the sentence below.
Remember to punctuate your answer correctly.

_____ asked me for directions to the library.

1 mark

47 Which verb completes the sentence so that it uses the **subjunctive form**?

If I _____ to find a treasure chest, I'd share it with you.

Tick **one**.

did ☐

was ☐

were ☐

had ☐

1 mark

48 Insert two **hyphens** in the correct places in the sentence below.

My mum, who is a well known author, has just written a new,

action packed book.

1 mark

49 Circle the **relative pronoun** in the sentence below.

When we reached the waterfall, which was our final destination,

we made our camp and settled down for the night.

1 mark

50 Use a **comma** and a **dash** in the correct places in the sentence below.

After we left the park we visited Ash and Paula the children who

live opposite you.

1 mark

SET
A

English
grammar,
punctuation
and spelling

PAPER 2

Key Stage 2

English grammar, punctuation and spelling

Paper 2: spelling

You will need to ask someone to read the instructions and sentences to you. These can be found on page 101.

Time:

You have approximately **15 minutes** to complete this test paper.

Maximum mark	Actual mark
20	

First name	
Last name	

Date of birth	Day		Month		Year	

Spelling

1 The actress performed _____ on stage.

2 Our _____ little kitten had scratched the carpet.

3 The flowers in the bathroom are _____.

4 The doctor said the rash was highly _____.

5 There is a _____ coming from the large window.

6 The weather is very _____ today.

7 The car in front was _____ right.

8 James's dad is a very _____ sailor.

9 Sam won a _____ he entered at school.

10 I think I have done _____ homework now.

11 Mangoes, pineapples, kiwis and oranges are all types of _____.

12 Raj was _____ shocked to see his old friend again.

13 The hotel sign said there was no _____.

14 It is a year since Auntie Jan and Uncle Paddy were _____.

15 The new _____ has introduced some interesting dishes.

16 Grace passed the _____ carefully to Dan.

17 I was very careful not to _____ my teacher's name.

18 We _____ ran for help when we heard the alarm.

19 Eventually, the _____ blew the final whistle.

20 Our family eats _____ for breakfast.

Key Stage 2

English reading

Reading answer booklet

Time:

You have **one hour** to read the texts in the reading booklet (pages 85–92) and answer the questions in this answer booklet.

Maximum mark	Actual mark
50	

First name	
Last name	

Date of birth	Day		Month		Year	

1 Write **two** phrases the author uses to create a magical setting in the first paragraph.

1. _____

2. _____ 1 mark

2 Look at the paragraph beginning: *Almost without knowing what he was doing, as though drawn by some powerful magnet . . .*

What do the words *as though drawn by some powerful magnet* tell you?

_____

_____ 1 mark

3 *The tunnel was damp and **murky** . . .*

Which word is closest in meaning to *murky*?

Tick **one**.

muddy ☐

gloomy ☐

soggy ☐

filthy ☐ 1 mark

4 What evidence is there to suggest that James was not frightened as he crawled through the tunnel?

_____

_____

5 *The creatures, some sitting on chairs, others reclining on a sofa, were all watching him **intently**.*

Which word is closest in meaning to *intently*?

Tick **one**.

casually ☐

closely ☐

quickly ☐

strangely ☐

6 Draw a line to match each creature to the description James gives when he first meets them.

Old-Green-Grasshopper ●	● giant
Spider ●	● enormous
Silkworm ●	● as large as a large dog
Ladybird ●	● thick and white

1 mark

© 2018 Letts Educational, an imprint of HarperCollinsPublishers Ltd – not to be photocopied.   **39**

7 *He glanced behind him, thinking he could bolt back into the tunnel . . .*

What does the word *bolt* tell you about how James is feeling?

_____

_____

2 marks

8 Give **two** reasons why you think that the creatures might eat James.

1. _____

2. _____

2 marks

9 Explain as fully as you can what the Ladybird means when she tells James,
'You are one of us now, didn't you know that?'

_____

_____

1 mark

10 Put a tick in the correct box to show whether each of the following statements is **true** or **false**.

	True	False
A fence surrounded the peach.		
The tunnel was dry and cold.		
James bumped his head on the stone in the middle of the peach.		
James couldn't stand up because the peach wasn't big enough.		
The creatures were at least the same size as James.		

1 mark

11 What **effect** is the author trying to create in the sentence below?

Four pairs of round black glassy eyes were all fixed upon James.

_____

_____

_____

_____

2 marks

12 Explain why this statement by the Centipede is funny.

And meanwhile I wish you'd come over here and give me a hand with these boots. It takes me hours to get them all off by myself.

_____

_____

_____

1 mark

13 Re-read to the end of the extract from the paragraph beginning *The Spider (who happened to be a female spider)*... on page 88.

What do you think James is thinking as the creatures talk?

_____

_____

_____

_____

3 marks

14 Why did Floella find growing up in South London challenging?

_____

_____ 1 mark

15 Look at the first paragraph.

Find and **copy one** word that is closest in meaning to 'move away'.

_____ 1 mark

16 Look at page 89.

How can you tell that Floella had a good relationship with her parents?

Give **three** pieces of evidence from the text.

1. _____

_____

2. _____

_____

3. _____

_____ 3 marks

17 What is the name of the first TV programme in which Floella starred?

_____

18 Find the year when each of the events below happened in Floella Benjamin's life. Write the answers in the grid below.

Event	Date
Born	
Came to England	
Made her TV debut	
Started her own television production company	
Wrote *Coming to England*	
Trekked the Great Wall of China	

19 In what order is the text written?

Tick **one**.

in order of importance ☐

in no particular order ☐

in chronological order ☐

1 mark

20 In her book *Coming to England,* Floella talks about her feelings of rejection.

Why do you think Floella felt rejected?

_____

_____

1 mark

21 Why is it a special achievement that Floella has run ten London Marathons?

_____

_____

1 mark

22 Look at the last paragraph on page 90.

Which word tells us that Floella understands and shares the feelings of children?

_____

23 Summarise **three** ways that Floella has helped children's charities.

1. _____

_____

2. _____

_____

3. _____

_____

24 Put a tick in the correct box to show whether each of the following statements about Floella is **fact** or **opinion**.

	Fact	Opinion
She worked in a bank.		
She loved her job on *Play School*.		
She presented *Play School* for 12 years.		
She has completed ten London Marathons.		
She is a keen runner.		

1 mark

25 Explain how Floella Benjamin's childhood influenced her to help young people across the world.

_____

_____

_____

_____   2 marks

26 *Macavity's a Mystery Cat: he's called the Hidden Paw —*

*For he's the master criminal who can **defy** the Law.*

Which word is closest in meaning to *defy*?

Tick **one**.

follow ☐

understand ☐

challenge ☐

attack ☐

1 mark

27 Why is Macavity the bafflement of Scotland Yard and the despair of the Flying Squad?

_____

_____

1 mark

28 The writer tells us that Macavity *breaks the law of gravity.*

What **two different** meanings are implied by this statement?

1. _____

_____

2. _____

_____

2 marks

29 Look at the third verse.

This verse tells readers more information about Macavity's ...

Tick one.

friends. ☐

personality. ☐

hobbies. ☐

appearance. ☐

1 mark

30 Look at the third verse.

Which word tells you that Macavity is uncared for?

_____

1 mark

31 Why do you think the poet repeats the words 'Macavity's not there'?

_____

_____

_____

1 mark

32 Put a tick in the correct box to show whether each of the following statements is **fact** or **opinion**.

	Fact	Opinion
It is fun watching Macavity cause trouble.		
Macavity's a ginger cat.		
His coat is dusty.		
Macavity has no-one to care for him.		

2 marks

33 What does the poem tell you about Macavity's character?

Describe **three** features of his character, using evidence from the text to support your answer.

_____

_____

_____

_____

_____

_____

3 marks

34 Do you think the writer feels admiration or contempt for Macavity?

Use evidence from the text in your answer.

_____

_____

_____

_____

_____

2 marks

SET
B

English
grammar,
punctuation
and spelling

PAPER 1

Key Stage 2

English grammar, punctuation and spelling

Paper 1: questions

E GPAS

Time:

You have **45 minutes** to complete this test paper.

Maximum mark	Actual mark
50	

First name	Jack				
Last name	Gray				
Date of birth	Day	16	Month	may	Year	2012

1   Circle the **adjectives** in the sentence below.

The mysterious shadows darted quickly along the creepy path.

1 mark

2   Which word completes the sentence below?

You cannot go on the field today _____ it is too muddy.

Tick **one**.

however ☐

although ☐

because  ✓

but ☐

1 mark

3   Insert an **apostrophe** in the correct place in each sentence to indicate possession.

The dogs tail was wagging.

Six boys coats were on the floor.

1 mark

4 Rewrite the sentence below so that it begins with the **adverbial**. Use only the same words and remember to punctuate your answer correctly.

Kenzie blew out the candles after the singing.

_____

_____

1 mark

5 Insert a **colon** in the correct place in the sentence below.

Mum put the following in my packed lunch cheese sandwiches, an apple and a yoghurt.

1 mark

6 Which sentence is punctuated correctly?

Tick **one.**

Grace found a bouncy ball; in the garden she was fairly sure it was Jamal's.

☐

Grace found a bouncy ball in the garden; she was fairly sure it was Jamal's.

☐

Grace found a bouncy ball in the garden she was fairly sure; it was Jamal's.

☐

Grace found a bouncy ball in the garden she was fairly; sure it was Jamal's.

☐

1 mark

7 The **prefix** dis– can be added to the word <u>approve</u> to make the word <u>disapprove</u>.

What does the word <u>disapprove</u> mean?

Tick **one**.

to make a mistake ☐

to find something unacceptable ☐

to prove something is right ☐

to think something is great ☐

1 mark

8 Write a suitable **modal verb** in the sentence below.

They really _____ take more care.

1 mark

9 Complete the sentence below with a **noun** formed from the verb <u>celebrate</u>.

We all joined in the _____ of the team's victory.

1 mark

10 Circle the **conjunction** in the sentence below.

The girls were tired but it was too early to go to bed.

1 mark

11 Circle the **object** in the sentence below.

The postman has just delivered this letter for you.

1 mark

12 Underline the **relative clause** in the sentence below.

The ice cream van that is in the car park is very popular today.

1 mark

13 Which two sentences below contain a **preposition**?

Tick **two**.

The truck drove under the bridge. ☐

Max dropped his ice cream so Mum bought him another. ☐

My best friend's uncle is a famous musician. ☐

Mum and I strolled along the canal path. ☐

1 mark

14 Write the name of a punctuation mark that could be used instead of brackets in the sentence below.

The trees (by now bent double by the relentless wind) stood little chance of surviving the storm.

_____

1 mark

15 Complete the sentence using suitable **pronouns**.

Rosie's homework was too hard for _____ and

_____ felt sad that _____

couldn't do it.

16 Which of the events in the sentences below is the **most** likely to happen?

Tick **one**.

We might go to the cinema tonight. ☐

He will go to school tomorrow. ☐

They could go camping at the weekend. ☐

I ought to tidy my bedroom. ☐

17 Which sentence is an **exclamation**?

Tick **one**.

I can't wait for the summer holidays ☐

I really love reading adventure books ☐

What a brilliant book that was ☐

What sort of books do you like reading ☐

18   Insert **a pair of brackets** in the correct place in the sentence below.

Mrs Jones the Year 5 teacher played the piano in school today.

19   Which underlined group of words is a **subordinate clause**?

Tick **one**.

Last Wednesday, I went to see my cousins. ☐

My friend Lauren is coming to stay the night. ☐

The flowers that Dad bought for Mum are
purple, white and blue. ☐

Dad is going fishing even if it rains. ☐

20   Insert a **comma** in the correct place in the sentence below.

Hanging upside down the bat made loud noises as the night sky
grew darker.

21   Complete the table by inserting suitable **antonyms**.

Word	Antonym
stiff	
angry	

22 What is the **word class** of each underlined word?

The monkeys <u>noisily</u> ate their food. _____

The monkeys made a lot of <u>noise</u> as they
ate their food. _____ 1 mark

23 Which sentence is a **statement**?

Tick **one**.

Ben has a new puppy called Sid ☐

Do you have any pets ☐

How I'd love to have a puppy ☐

Be careful how you hold the puppy ☐ 1 mark

24 Which one **prefix** can be added to all three words below to make their antonyms?
Write the prefix in the box.

behave

place

understand

☐ 1 mark

25 Write **two conjunctions** to complete the sentence below.

I like drawing _____ painting

_____ my sister prefers writing. 1 mark

26 Rewrite the sentence below so that it begins with the **adverbial**.
Remember to punctuate your sentence correctly.

We went to the cinema after tea.

_____

1 mark

27 Complete the sentence below with the **simple past tense** of the verbs
in boxes.

Mrs Shepherd _____ her class that the visitor

to tell

who _____ in assembly last year _____ this morning's

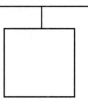

to speak

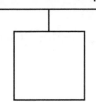

to be

special guest.

1 mark

28 Label each of the clauses in the sentence below as either **main** (M)
or **subordinate** (S).

As we were walking to school,   we saw Angus   who was with his parents.

1 mark

29 Explain how the position of the apostrophe changes the meaning of
the second sentence.

1. Have you bought the singer's latest CDs?

2. Have you bought the singers' latest CDs?

_____

_____

_____

1 mark

30 Rewrite the sentence below in the **active**.
Remember to punctuate your answer correctly.

The hedges were cut by some hard-working gardeners.

_____

1 mark

31 Tick one box in each row to show whether the underlined noun is **singular** or **plural**.

	Singular	Plural
The <u>children's</u> artwork was displayed in the main corridor.		
Our <u>dogs'</u> biggest excitement of the day is the morning walk.		
My <u>class's</u> main claim to fame is that we have three sets of twins.		

1 mark

32 Insert a **pair of commas** in the correct place in the sentence below.

My grandfather always kind and understanding told me that

he would help me with my tricky homework.

1 mark

33 Which of the sentences below uses the **semi-colon** correctly?

Tick **one**.

Ella played the piano; Alex played the flute.   ☐

Ella played; the piano Alex played; the flute.   ☐

Ella played; the piano; Alex played the flute.   ☐

Ella; played the piano Alex; played the flute.   ☐

1 mark

34 What is the **subject** of the sentence below?

Every summer, Moira goes with her brother to Scotland.

Tick **one**.

summer ☐

Moira ☐

brother ☐

Scotland ☐

1 mark

35 Which sentence is the most **formal**?

Tick **one**.

What time does the get-together kick off later? ☐

The walkers are required to wear waterproofs should it rain. ☐

Let's get a move on or we shall be late! ☐

There's a great film on at the cinema tonight. ☐

1 mark

36 Underline the **relative clause** in the sentence below.

Brighton, which is a seaside town, is located on the south coast of England.

1 mark

37 Rewrite the sentence below as **direct speech**.
Remember to punctuate your sentence correctly.

The children asked the teacher if they could have some extra playtime.

_____

_____

1 mark

38 Which sentence is punctuated correctly?

Tick **one**.

Liam is determined – to win this year's tennis tournament he's practised day and night.

☐

Liam is determined to win this year's tennis tournament – he's practised day and night.

☐

Liam is determined to win this year's tennis tournament he's practised – day and night.

☐

Liam is determined to win – this year's tennis tournament he's practised day and night.

☐

1 mark

39 Replace the underlined words in the sentences below with their **contracted forms**.

They <u>should have</u> realised <u>we had</u> taken the dog out when he <u>was not</u> on his mat.

↑	↑	↑

1 mark

40 Insert the correct punctuation into this sentence.
The first one has been done for you.

D
~~d~~uring his stay on the farm jon saw some ducks a herd of goats and a huge pink pig

1 mark

41 Circle the **possessive pronoun** in the passage below.

I handed my form into the teacher. Fergus has lost his so

he has been given another one.

1 mark

42 Rewrite the sentence below using **Standard English**.

I've not got none.

_____

1 mark

43 Circle each word that should begin with a capital letter in the sentence below.

last saturday, I went to a museum in edinburgh,

the capital of scotland, with my uncle.

44 Add a **suffix** to each verb below to make a **noun**.

Verb	Noun
agree	
assist	

45 Which punctuation mark should be used in the place indicated by the arrow?

Dad is anxious to get to work early this morning↑ he will hear whether

he has been promoted or not!

Tick **one**.

comma ☐

hyphen ☐

semi-colon ☐

apostrophe ☐

46 Insert a **comma** and a **dash** in the correct places in the sentence below.

As soon as we reached the cottage Mum and Dad lit a

fire it was cold even for spring.

47 Rewrite the underlined verbs in the sentences below so that they are in the **present progressive form.**

Mum <u>teaches</u> yoga at the village hall.

She <u>intends</u> to teach me some exercises.

48 Complete each sentence below with a word formed from the **root word** <u>kind</u>.

Kai showed great _____ when he helped the boy cross the road.

Our neighbour _____ looked after our dog when we went away.

1 mark

49 Insert an **apostrophe** to show possession in the sentence below.

Annies mum worked at the school library.

1 mark

50 Which word completes the sentence so that it uses the **subjunctive mood?**

The Head Teacher said, "If there _____ to be a fire, students should exit through the rear doors."

Tick **one.**

was ☐

were ☐

had ☐

going ☐

1 mark

Key Stage 2

English grammar, punctuation and spelling

Paper 2: spelling

You will need to ask someone to read the instructions and sentences to you. These can be found on pages 101–102.

Time:

You have approximately **15 minutes** to complete this test paper.

Maximum mark	Actual mark
20	

First name	
Last name	

Date of birth	Day		Month		Year	

Spelling

1 Bea greeted the new member _____ .

2 Gran likes _____ during the long, winter months.

3 My ambition is to play football for my _____.

4 The chocolate cake was _____.

5 The _____ of Majorca is close to Spain.

6 The weather promises to be quite _____ this weekend.

7 You _____ you wouldn't tell.

8 We do not mind what type of _____ we stay in on holiday.

9 _____ can be mashed, chipped, boiled or baked.

10 After a _____ search, we still couldn't find the keys.

11 We spoke _____ to the hysterical girl.

12 Coffee and fizzy drinks usually contain _____.

13 A visiting _____ played his guitar in assembly.

14 Our teacher is good at _____ with our parents.

15 My _____ feels full after lunch.

16 Everyone has _____ fingerprints.

17 We are always _____ when we walk down the cliff steps.

18 Ned's _____ was the fastest.

19 The gymnasts _____ their weight across the bars.

20 The whole family is in _____ for our pet.

**THIS PAGE HAS INTENTIONALLY
BEEN LEFT BLANK**

**THIS PAGE HAS INTENTIONALLY
BEEN LEFT BLANK**

**THIS PAGE HAS INTENTIONALLY
BEEN LEFT BLANK**

**THIS PAGE HAS INTENTIONALLY
BEEN LEFT BLANK**

Contents

English reading booklets

**THIS PAGE HAS INTENTIONALLY
BEEN LEFT BLANK**

Reading booklet

Contents

A Mad Tea Party

Alice has just drunk a magic potion, which has made her very small. It enables her to enter Wonderland, where nothing is ever quite as it seems!

The scene begins in the garden. There is a table under a tree in front of a house. The March Hare and the Hatter are having tea at the table. A dormouse sits between them.

Narrator: The March Hare and the Mad Hatter are having tea, all squashed at one end of a very large table.

Alice: Hello, mind if I join you all?

Hare, Hatter, Dormouse: No room! No room!

Alice: What are you talking about, there's plenty of room.

Alice sits down.

Hare: Have some wine.

Alice: *(looking around the table)* I don't see any wine.

Hare: There isn't any.

Alice: *(in an angry voice)* Then it wasn't very civil of you to offer it!

Hare: It wasn't very civil of you to sit down without being invited.

Alice: I didn't know it was your table; it's laid for many more than three.

Hatter: *(looking up and down at Alice)* Your hair wants cutting.

Alice: You should learn not to make personal remarks. It's very rude!

Narrator: The characters continue arguing until the Hatter opens his eyes very wide and begins talking in riddles.

Hatter: Why is a raven like a writing desk?

Alice: I believe I can guess that.

Hare: Do you mean you think you can find the answer for it?

Alice: Exactly so.

Hare: Then you should say what you mean.

Alice: I do. At least, I mean what I say – that's the same thing you know.

Hatter: Not the same thing a bit! Why, you might just as well say that I like what I get is the same as I get what I like.

Dormouse: *(talking in a sleepy way)* I breathe when I sleep is the same thing as I sleep when I breathe!

Hatter: It is the same thing with you!

Narrator: The conversation drops, and the party sits silently for a minute.

(The Hatter takes his watch out of his pocket and looks at it uneasily; he shakes it and holds it to his ear. He then dips it in his cup of tea and looks at it again.)

Hatter: What day of the month is it?

Alice: *(thinks for a time)* The fourth.

Hatter: *(looking angrily at the March Hare)* Two days wrong! I told you butter wouldn't suit the works!

Hare: *(meekly)* It was the *best* butter.

Hatter: Yes, but some crumbs must have got in as well. You shouldn't have put it in with the bread-knife.

Alice: What a funny watch! It tells the day of the month, and doesn't tell what o'clock it is!

The Isles of Scilly

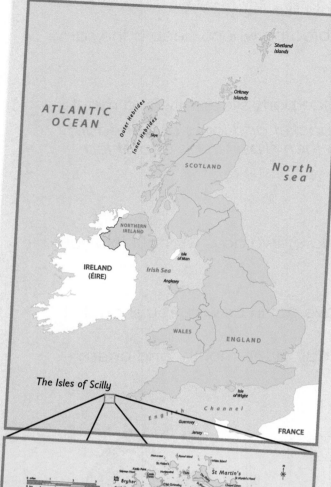

Location

The Isles of Scilly are a group of islands located 45 km (28 miles) off the coast of the Cornish peninsula.

The Islands

The Isles of Scilly are made up of five inhabited and approximately 140 other islands. The largest of the islands is called St Mary's, with Tresco, St Martin's, St Agnes and Bryher being the others.

The main settlement on St Mary's is Hugh Town. This is a very small town with only a few shops, banks, restaurants, hotels and pubs. The population of Hugh Town is just over 1000.

Travel

Because the Isles of Scilly are so small, very few people own cars. Locals usually walk or ride bicycles. Public transport is a boat service between the islands.

To reach the Isles of Scilly from the mainland, visitors need to travel on either a small aeroplane (Skybus) or a passenger ferry (*The Scillonian*). These methods of transport are both an amazing experience for travellers to the islands and the table below lists the advantages and disadvantages of each.

	Skybus	The Scillonian
Advantages	Travel to and from three different mainland airports	Cafés serving hot and cold food on board
	Bird's-eye views of the islands	Often see dolphins, sea birds and basking sharks
	Quick	Seaside views
	Small and personal	Cheap
Disadvantages	Limited luggage allowed	Often rough seas and passengers may suffer motion sickness
	More expensive	Longer journey
	Flights can be cancelled because of high winds	

Weather

The Isles of Scilly have a unique climate, with the mildest and warmest temperatures in the United Kingdom. The average annual temperature is 11.8 °C (53.2 °F) in comparison to London, where it is 11.6 °C (52.9 °F).

The winters in Scilly are relatively warm and the islands very rarely get frosts or snow. They are however windy, due to the full force of the wind off the Atlantic Ocean.

Plants and Animals

The warm, humid climate of the Isles of Scilly allows a variety of rare plants and flowers to grow, which are not seen in other parts of the United Kingdom.

Some people describe the Scilly Islands as 'a large, natural greenhouse'. Even in winter, there are hundreds of different plants in bloom.

Month	Jan	Feb	Mar	Apr	May	Jun	Jul	Aug	Sept	Oct	Nov	Dec
Average temp. °C (°F)	8.0 (46.4)	7.9 (46.2)	8.8 (47.8)	9.8 (49.6)	12.0 (53.5)	14.5 (58.1)	16.5 (61.7)	16.9 (62.5)	15.5 (59.8)	12.7 (54.8)	10.3 (50.6)	8.7 (47.6)

Because of the warm temperatures, many birds migrate to Scilly. Some birds stop off on their way across the Atlantic Ocean, while others stay on the islands. There are many different types of birds on the islands, ranging from common birds such as sparrows, thrushes and gulls, to more unusual birds like puffins, cuckoos and wheatears.

Tourism

The Isles of Scilly rely on tourism. The majority of shops, restaurants, bars and cafés earn money from visitors during the summer season. People travel to Scilly for many reasons. Quite often there are visitors who come on walking holidays, bird-watching trips and to relax on one of the quiet beaches.

Holidaymakers can choose accommodation suitable for their stay. The main islands have a choice of hotels, bed and breakfasts, self-catering cottages and camping facilities.

Activities

Many people choose to participate in water sports, including sailing, kayaking, boating and fishing.

The islands are famous for their clear waters, which also make snorkelling and diving popular activities.

'Gig racing' is the main sport on the Isles of Scilly. Gigs are traditional working boats, which six or seven people sit inside and row. Many islanders take part in gig practices and races throughout the season.

People watch the races and cheer on the gigs from passenger boats that follow the race or they sometimes watch the finish from the quay on St Mary's. The Isles of Scilly host an annual gig championship; thousands of rowers from as far away as Holland flock to the island to race at this event.

Historic Sites

The Isles of Scilly have many historic landmarks waiting to be explored, including castles, churches, lighthouses and ruins. There are art galleries and exhibitions, museums and often concerts to attend.

Probably the most impressive feature of the Isles of Scilly is its natural beauty; the swirling golden beaches, sand dunes, rocky coastlines and scenic views are well worth a visit.

Street Child

'Joseph,' Jim asked the bent man one day out in the yard. 'How long have you been here?'

'Been here?' Joseph swung his head round and peered up at Jim. 'Seems like I was born here. Don't know nothing else, son. And I don't know all of this place neither.' He leaned against Jim so he could swing his head up to look at the long, high building with its rows of barred windows. 'I've not been in the room where the women go, though long ago I must have been in the baby-room, I suppose, with my ma. I've been in the infirmary wards. But there's all kinds of little twisty corridors and attics and places I've never been in Jim, and I don't want to, neither. It's the whole world, this place is.' He spread out his hands. 'Whole world.'

'It ain't, Joseph,' Jim told him. 'There's no shops here, and no carriages. And no trees.' He closed his eyes, forcing himself to try and remember what it was like outside. 'And there's no river. There's a great big river outside here.'

'Is there now?' said Joseph. 'I should like to see that river. Though to tell you the truth, Jim, I don't know what a river is. Tell you something.' He put his arm over Jim's shoulder to draw his ear closer to his own mouth. 'I don't want to die in here. If someone will let me know what day I'm going to die, I'll be grateful. I'll climb over that wall first.' He dropped his head down again and stared at his boots, whistling softly. 'Yes. That's what I'll do.'

Tip spluttered and nudged Jim, but Jim was looking up at the high walls that surrounded the workhouse, and at the bleak sky above it.

'How long have I been here, Tip?' he asked.

'How should I know?' Tip hugged his arms round himself. 'Keep moving, Jim. It's cold.'

It was impossible to tell one day from the next. They were all the same. School, sack-making, bed. The only thing that changed was the sky. Jim had seen the grey of snow clouds turning into the soft rain clouds of spring. He'd felt summer scorching him in his heavy, itchy clothes. And now the sky was steely grey again. The pump had long beards of ice on its handle.

'I've been here a year,' Jim said. It was then that the little secret promise that had nestled inside him began to flutter into life like a wild thing.

'I've got to skip off,' he let the mad thought rise up in him.

'If I don't, I'll be like Joseph. One day I won't remember whether I was born here or not. I won't know anywhere but here.'

During lessons that day, the old schoolmaster's voice droned on in the dim schoolroom. The boys coughed and shuffled in their benches, hunching themselves against the cold. Jim's wild thoughts drummed inside him, so loud that he imagined everyone would hear them. He leaned over to Tip and whispered in his ear, 'Tip, I'm going to run away today. Come with me?' Tip sheered round, and put his hand to his mouth. Mr Barrack sprang down from his chair, his eyes alight with anger and joy.

'You spoke!' he said to Jim, triumphant. 'It was you.'

Tip closed his eyes and held out his hand, but Jim stood up. He didn't mind. He didn't mind anything any more. The teacher hauled him off his stool and swung his rope round. It hummed as it sliced through the air.

'I don't mind,' Jim tried to explain, but this made Mr Barrack angrier than ever. At last he had caught Jim out, and he was beating him now for every time he had tried and failed. He pulled a greasy handkerchief out of his pocket and wound it round Jim's head, tying it tight under his chin.

'Just in case you feels like hollering,' he said. All the other boys stared in front of them. The rope stung Jim again and again and the beating inside him was like a wild bird now, throbbing in his limbs and in his stomach, in his chest and in his head, so wild and loud that he felt it would lift him up and carry him away.

When the schoolmaster had finished with him he flung him like a bundle of rags across the desk. Jim lay in a shimmer of pain and thrumming wings. He wanted to sleep. The bell rang and the boys shuffled out. Jim felt Tip's hand on his shoulder. He flinched away.

'That's what they do to the boys who skip off, Jim,' Tip whispered. 'They thrash 'em like that every day until they are good.'

Jim felt the wild thing fluttering again. 'Only if they catch them.'

'They always catch 'em. Bobbies catch 'em and bring 'em in, and they get thrashed and thrashed.'

Jim struggled to sit up. The stinging rolled down his body. 'Won't you come with me?'

'I daresn't. Honest, I daresn't. Don't go, Jim.'

Jim looked up at the great archways of the schoolroom. He knew the words off by heart. *God is good. God is holy. God is just. God is love.*

'I've got to,' he said. 'And I'm going tonight, Tip.'

Jim knew that he would have to make his break before old Marion did her rounds for the night. He had no idea how he was going to do it. At suppertime he stuffed his cheese in his pocket, and Tip passed his own share along to him.

At the end of the meal, Mr Sissons stood up on his dais. All the shuffling and whispering stopped. He moved his body slowly round, which was his way of fixing his eyes on everyone, freezing them like statues.

'I'm looking for some big boys,' he said. 'To help with the carpet-beaters.' He waited in silence, but nobody moved.

'Just as I would expect. A rush to help, when there is sickness in the wards.' A cold sigh seemed to ripple through the room. Mr Sissons laughed into it in his dry, hissing way. 'It might be cholera, my dears. That's what I hear. I've two thousand mouths to feed here, and someone has to earn the money, cholera or not. Somebody has to buy the medicines. Somebody has to pay for the burials.' He moved his body round in its slow, watchful circle again. 'Plenty of big strong boys here, eating every crumb I give them and never a word of thanks.' He stepped down from his dais and

walked along the rows, cuffing boys on the back of their heads as he passed them. 'I want you all up in the women's wards straight after supper, and you don't come down again till all the carpets are done.'

'What's carpets?' asked Jim.

'Dunno,' Tip whispered, 'they come from the rich houses, and the women here beat 'em, and then they send them home.'

'I'm going with them,' Jim said suddenly, standing up as soon as the older boys did.

'A daft boy, you are,' said Tip. 'He asked for big boys.'

'You coming or not?' Jim darted off after the big boys and Tip ran after him.

Reading booklet

Contents

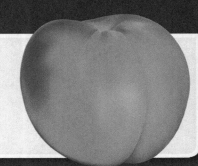

James and the Giant Peach

The garden lay soft and silver in the moonlight. The grass was wet with dew and a million dewdrops were sparkling and twinkling like diamonds around his feet. And now suddenly, the whole place, the whole garden seemed to be *alive* with magic.

Almost without knowing what he was doing, as though drawn by some powerful magnet, James Henry Trotter started walking slowly towards the giant peach. He climbed over the fence that surrounded it, and stood directly beneath it, staring up at its great bulging sides. He put out a hand and touched it gently with the tip of one finger. It felt soft and warm and slightly furry, like the skin of a baby mouse. He moved a step closer and rubbed his cheek lightly against the soft skin. And then suddenly, while he was doing this, he happened to notice that right beside him and below him, close to the ground, there was a hole in the side of the peach.

It was quite a large hole, the sort of thing an animal about the size of a fox might have made.

James knelt down in front of it and poked his head and shoulders inside.

He crawled in.

He kept on crawling.

This isn't just a hole, he thought excitedly. It's a tunnel!

The tunnel was damp and murky, and all around him there was the curious bittersweet smell of fresh peach. The floor was soggy under his knees, the walls were wet and sticky, and peach juice was dripping from the ceiling. James opened his mouth and caught some of it on his tongue. It tasted delicious.

He was crawling uphill now, as though the tunnel were leading straight towards the very centre of the gigantic fruit. Every few seconds he paused and took a bite out of the wall. The peach flesh was sweet and juicy, and marvellously refreshing.

He crawled on for several more yards, and then suddenly – bang – the top of his head

bumped into something extremely hard blocking his way. He glanced up. In front of him there was a solid wall that seemed at first as though it were made of wood. He touched it with his fingers. It certainly felt like wood, except that it was very jagged and full of deep grooves.

'Good heavens!' he said. 'I know what this is! I've come to the stone in the middle of the peach!'

Then he noticed that there was a small door cut into the face of the peach stone. He gave a push. It swung open. He crawled through it, and before he had time to glance up and see where he was, he heard a voice saying, 'Look who's here!' And another one said, 'We've been waiting for you!'

James stopped and stared at the speakers, his face white with horror.

He started to stand up, but his knees were shaking so much he had to sit down again on the floor. He glanced behind him, thinking he could bolt back into the tunnel the way he had come, but the doorway had disappeared. There was now only a solid brown wall behind him.

James's large frightened eyes travelled slowly around the room.

The creatures, some sitting on chairs, others reclining on a sofa, were all watching him intently.

Creatures?

Or were they insects?

An insect is usually something rather small, is it not? A grasshopper, for example, is an insect.

So what would you call it if you saw a grasshopper as large as a dog? As large as a *large* dog. You could hardly call *that* an insect, could you?

There was an Old-Green-Grasshopper as large as a large dog sitting on a stool directly across the room from James now.

And next to the Old-Green-Grasshopper, there was an enormous Spider.

And next to the Spider, there was a giant Ladybird with nine black spots on her scarlet shell.

Each of these three was squatting upon a magnificent chair.

On a sofa near by, reclining comfortably in curled-up positions, there was a Centipede and an Earthworm.

On the floor over in the far corner, there was something thick and white that looked as though it might be a Silkworm. But it was sleeping soundly and nobody was paying any attention to it.

Every one of these 'creatures' was at least as big as James himself, and in the strange greenish light that shone down from somewhere in the ceiling, they were absolutely terrifying to behold.

'I'm hungry!' the Spider announced suddenly, staring hard at James.

'I'm famished!' the Old-Green-Grasshopper said.

'So am *I*!' the Ladybird cried.

The Centipede sat up a little straighter on the sofa. *'Everyone's* famished!' he said. 'We need food!'

Four pairs of round black glassy eyes were all fixed upon James.

The Centipede made a wriggling movement with his body as though he were about to glide off the sofa — but he didn't.

There was a long pause — and a long silence.

The Spider (who happened to be a female spider) opened her mouth and ran a long black tongue delicately over her lips. 'Aren't you hungry?' she asked suddenly, leaning forward and addressing herself to James.

Poor James was backed up against the far wall, shivering with fright and much too terrified to answer.

'What's the matter with you?' the Old-Green-Grasshopper asked. 'You look positively ill!'

'He looks as though he's going to faint any second,' the Centipede said.

'Oh, my goodness, the poor thing!' the Ladybird cried. 'I do believe he thinks it's *him* that we are wanting to eat!' There was a roar of laughter from all sides.

'Oh dear, oh dear!' they said. 'What an awful thought!'

'You mustn't be frightened,' the Ladybird said kindly. 'We wouldn't dream of hurting you. You are one of us now, didn't you know that? You are one of the crew. We're all in the same boat.'

'We've been waiting for you all day long,' the Old-Green-Grasshopper said. 'We thought you were never going to turn up. I'm glad you made it.'

'So cheer up, my boy, cheer up!' the Centipede said. 'And meanwhile I wish you'd come over here and give me a hand with these boots. It takes me *hours* to get them all off by myself.'

About Floella

Floella Benjamin was born in the Caribbean on an island called Trinidad on 23rd September 1949. Her father decided to emigrate to England and she came to join him in 1960, when she was 11 years old. Floella's family started their life in Great Britain in Beckenham, South London. Initially she found it very different to her life in Trinidad and growing up in two cultures was challenging.

Floella's mother (Marmie) was a great inspiration to her. She gave her lots of love and encouraged her to do well at school.

Floella always dreamed of becoming a teacher, but instead ended up working in a bank and then later starred in stage musicals. While Floella enjoyed being on stage, she also wanted to try working in television so she auditioned for a variety of roles. Her TV debut was in 1974 in a drama called *Within these Walls* and her success in the show landed her many more roles in TV dramas.

Floella then took on a new role as a presenter of *Play School*, a 1970s children's show. She loved this job and presented the programme for 12 years.

As well as acting and presenting, Floella also loves to sing. She began singing with her dad who had a jazz band.

She often sang with her dad's band and also with large classical orchestras.

In 1987 Floella started her own television production company.

Next page ▶▶▶

Floella has also starred in several pantomimes, worked on numerous radio programmes, narrated audio books and has done voiceovers for a range of adverts and commercials.

Since 1983, Floella has written over 25 children's books.

One book Floella is particularly proud of is one that has been made into a film. *Coming to England* was written in 1995 and is based on her own life. In the book Floella talks about what it's like to be different, to move countries and change cultures and her feelings of rejection. The drama *Coming to England* won a Royal Television Society Award in 2004.

Floella is a keen runner who has completed ten London Marathons for the children's charity Barnardo's. This achievement is even more special as until she turned 50 years old, Floella had never even run at all!

Trekking the Great Wall of China in 2004 in aid of NCH Action for Children is another one of Floella's achievements. She started this in the Gobi Desert and finished 400 km later where the Great Wall meets the Yellow Sea.

Today Floella's passion is for inspiring and helping children and young people. She is a patron and supporter of many charities, including Action for Children and the Sickle Cell Society. In 2008, Floella was inducted into the National Society for the Prevention of Cruelty to Children (NSPCC) Hall of Fame.

Floella supports and empathises with children and young people across the world. Through her charity work, her writing and personal attitudes, she strives to help young people find their identity and to understand where they come from. She hopes all children have a sense of belonging and learn to become proud of themselves.

Macavity

Macavity's a Mystery Cat: he's called the Hidden Paw –
    For he's the master criminal who can defy the Law.
He's the bafflement of Scotland Yard, the Flying Squad's despair:
    For when they reach the scene of crime – *Macavity's not there!*

Macavity, Macavity, there's no one like Macavity,
    He's broken every human law, he breaks the law of gravity.
His powers of levitation would make a fakir stare,
    And when you reach the scene of crime – Macavity's not there!
You may seek him in the basement, you may look up in the air –
    But I tell you once and once again, *Macavity's not there!*

Macavity's a ginger cat, he's very tall and thin;
    You would know him if you saw him, for his eyes are sunken in.
His brow is deeply lined with thought, his head is highly domed;
    His coat is dusty from neglect, his whiskers are uncombed.
He sways his head from side to side, with movements like a snake;
    And when you think he's half asleep, he's always wide awake.

Macavity, Macavity, there's no one like Macavity,
    For he's a fiend in feline shape, a monster of depravity.
You may meet him in a by-street, you may see him in the square –
    But when a crime's discovered, then *Macavity's not there!*

He's outwardly respectable. (They say he cheats at cards.)
    And his footprints are not found in any file of Scotland Yard's.
And when the larder's looted, or the jewel-case is rifled,
    Or when the milk is missing, or another Peke's been stifled,
Or the greenhouse glass is broken, and the trellis past repair –
    Ay, there's the wonder of the thing! *Macavity's not there!*

And when the Foreign Office find a Treaty's gone astray,
      Or the Admiralty lose some plans and drawings by the way,
There may be a scrap of paper in the hall or on the stair –
      But it's useless to investigate – *Macavity's not there!*
And when the loss has been disclosed, the Secret Service say:
      'It *must* have been Macavity!' – but he's a mile away.
You'll be sure to find him resting, or a-licking of his thumbs,
      Or engaged in doing complicated long division sums.

Macavity, Macavity, there's no one like Macavity,
      There never was a Cat of such deceitfulness and suavity.
He always has an alibi, and one or two to spare:
      At whatever time the deed took place – MACAVITY WASN'T THERE!
And they say that all the Cats whose wicked deeds are widely known,
      (I might mention Mungojerrie, I might mention Griddlebone)
Are nothing more than agents for the Cat who all the time
      Just controls their operations: the Napoleon of Crime!

Answers and mark scheme

Set A English reading

A Mad Tea Party

1. Accept either (at a table) in the garden or (at a table) in Wonderland. **(1 mark)**
2. She has just drunk a magic potion that makes her small. **(1 mark)**
3. …there's plenty of room. **(1 mark)**
4. the Hare **(1 mark)**
5. Because the Hare offers her some wine when there actually isn't any. **(1 mark)**
6. polite **(1 mark)**
7. ' …all squashed at one end of a very large table.' **(1 mark)**
8. Any one of the following points:
   - Alice thinks personal remarks are rude.
   - The Hatter's remarks are said very abruptly and to the point.
   - The Hatter's remarks are unprovoked.
   (1 mark)
9. Any one from: lessens; they become quiet; ends. **(1 mark)**
10. frustrated **(1 mark)**
11. Accept any suitable answer, e.g. He dips his watch in his cup of tea. **(1 mark)**
12. Any one from: it is a tea party which is very unusual; the characters are acting in strange ways; they are saying mad things; they are sitting squashed up; they are talking in riddles; they are offering wine which isn't there. **(1 mark)**
13. puzzle **(1 mark)**
14. Any one from: the Narrator sets the scene; moves the story forward; explains what's happening; introduces characters. **(1 mark)**
15. works **(1 mark)**
16. Because even the best butter wouldn't be good for your watch. **(1 mark)**

The Isles of Scilly

17. St Mary's **(1 mark)**
18. people live there **(1 mark)**
19. a small aeroplane (Skybus); a passenger ferry (*The Scillonian*)
    (1 mark for both correct)
20. A day visitor with no luggage would be best taking the aeroplane (Skybus) because it's quicker and they would have longer to spend in the Isles of Scilly. They have no luggage so can travel by aeroplane. They will get a good view of all the islands even though they will not get time to see them all on foot. They will be able to choose one of three airports to travel from on the mainland.
    (1 mark for any point from above)
    A family staying for a week who want to see dolphins swimming would be best taking the passenger ferry because they may be able to see dolphins (and basking sharks and sea birds) from the ferry. They are staying a whole week so have plenty of time to spend travelling to Scilly by boat. The family might want to buy food or drinks on board and, as the boat is cheaper, it will cost them less. They can take more luggage than in the aeroplane.
    (1 mark for any point from above)
21. Its warm, humid climate means that rare plants and flowers can grow, even in winter.
    (1 mark)
22. If there are high winds. **(1 mark)**
23. Participating: a participant would sit inside the gig; row; take part in races.
    Watching: a spectator would watch the race from a boat, or from the quay on St Mary's; cheer on the gigs.
    (2 marks: 1 mark for one participating point, 1 mark for one watching point)
24. Any three from: walking; bird watching; relaxing on beaches; water sports; visiting historic sites and art galleries; enjoying the wildlife / plants.
    (1 mark for three correct answers)
25. Any two from: walk; ride bicycles; by boat.
    (1 mark)
26. a travel leaflet **(1 mark)**
27. Accept any indication that the child understands that this phrase gives readers an image of the buildings waiting for people to visit them – really the buildings are just standing there – the author adds interest.
    (1 mark)

28.

Statement	True	False
Hugh Town is a big city with a large population.		✓
The Isles of Scilly are connected by bridges.		✓
There are many different types of birds on the islands.	✓	
Shops, restaurants, bars and cafés rely on tourism to make money.	✓	

(1 mark for all correct)

29. special **(1 mark)**

Street Child

30. They are like prison windows. **(1 mark)**

31. trees; shops; a river **(1 mark for all correct)**

32. Winter. Tip says it is cold; the pump had (long beards of) ice on its handle. **(2 marks)**

33. He could tell from the changing seasons. **(1 mark)**

34. His promise to himself to escape / run away. **(1 mark)**

35. pulled **(1 mark)**

36. Any one from: he knew he had plans to run away; he wasn't going to be there much longer, he had more important things to think about; this would be his last beating so he felt positive and thought he could deal with anything. **(1 mark)**

37. To stop him screaming / hollering (while he was being beaten / thrashed). **(1 mark)**

38. That he is as worthless as a bundle of rags; that he is as light as a bundle of rags. **(2 marks)**

39. He was afraid they'll get caught and get thrashed. **(1 mark)**

40. Any one from: there is no good, justice or love here; God is not looking after me **(1 mark)**

41. Any three from: Look out for each other: 'Don't go, Jim.' Care for each other: 'Tip passed his own share along to him.' Trust each other: Jim told Tip his plans – 'Tip, I'm going to run away today. Come with me?' Strong friendship: they suffer the workhouse together.
(3 marks: award 1 mark for each correct point)

42.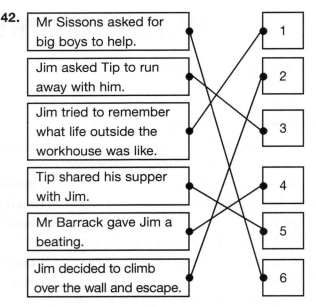

(1 mark for all correct)

43. joy; triumphant

(1 mark for either)

44. Answers may vary. Example:
The words used make me think Jim's thoughts were crazy and like a drum banging loudly in his head. **(1 mark)**

Set A English grammar, punctuation and spelling

Paper 1: questions

1. determiners **(1 mark)**
2. discover **(1 mark)**
3. We **was /** (were) going to play outside on our bikes.
   I **done /** (did) well in my maths test this morning. **(1 mark)**
4. "Wait for me!" shouted Orla. **(1 mark)**
5. were building **(1 mark)**
6. Put the flour and butter in the bowl. **(1 mark)**
7. ₙottingham is located in the ₑast ₘidlands. ₜhe river that runs through ₙottingham is called the river ₜrent. **(1 mark for all correct)**
8. It's been a long time since I've seen you, hasn't it **(1 mark)**

9.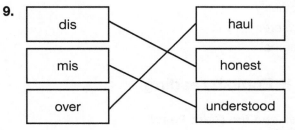
   (1 mark)

10. Emma's cat has had five kittens which are black, though one has white patches around its eyes; their neighbour's dog will now have six cats to chase! **(1 mark for both correct)**
11. The books **and** DVDs need returning to the library on Monday **or** Tuesday, **but** remember it is closed each day for lunch. **(1 mark for all correct)**
12. William Shakespeare – a famous author – wrote the play 'Macbeth'. **(1 mark)**
13. Although she is younger, my sister is much taller than me. **(1 mark)**

14.

Sentence	Present Progressive	Past progressive
While the band was playing, Jamie and I were dancing.		✓
We are reading about the Romans in history.	✓	
The bell is ringing so we must go inside.	✓	

(1 mark for all correct)

15. You've been learning about materials in science, **haven't you**? **(1 mark)**
16. We might go to the park later – it just depends on the weather. **(1 mark)**
17. Our classroom light keeps flickering on and off. **(1 mark)**
18. Feeling confident, the pianist played to a room full of people. **(1 mark)**
19. whipped **(1 mark)**
20. In the second sentence, it is not certain that William will wash the car. **(1 mark)**

21.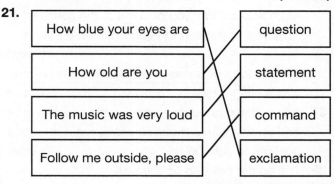
   (1 mark for all correct)

22. Answers will vary. Examples:
   "Is the tennis match on TV tonight?" asked Sami.
   Sami asked, "Is the tennis match on TV tonight?"
   (1 mark)
23. Later that evening, we said goodbye and began our journey home. **(1 mark)**
24. Mangoes, kiwis, apples, pineapples and strawberries are all types of fruit. **(1 mark for all correct)**
25. rang; came; told **(1 mark for all three correct)**
26. (dawn) (Sunrise) **(1 mark for both correct)**
27.

	Synonym	Antonym
sad	unhappy	happy
rich	wealthy	poor
big	large	small
old	ancient	new

(1 mark)

28. The skateboard park (located behind the playground) is to be used by children who are over eight. **(1 mark)**

29. (hard) **(1 mark)**

30. The historians visited the ancient ruins. **(1 mark)**

31. pronoun; possessive pronoun
    (1 mark for both correct)

32. calculator / calculation **(1 mark)**

33. (up) **(1 mark)**

34. (his) **(1 mark)**

35. Answers will vary. Examples:
    Mum asked, "Will you help me in the garden?"
    "Will you help me in the garden?" asked Mum.
    (1 mark)

36. The old lady who was shouting at her neighbour was feeling angry. **(1 mark)**

37. Any suitable question starting with a capital letter and ending with a question mark, e.g. How does Joel get to school? **(1 mark)**

38. The spider crawled up the wall.
    I put the spider in the garden.
    (1 mark for both correct)

39. he **(1 mark)**

40. Any one from: can't; won't; didn't; don't; couldn't; wouldn't **(1 mark)**

41. was dancing; were clapping
    (1 mark for both correct)

42. "What time does the train leave the station?" Mary asked the guard.
    "Three minutes past ten," the guard answered.
    (1 mark for both sentences correct)

43. semi-colon **(1 mark)**

44. While I was waiting to see the doctor, I read a book. **(1 mark)**

45. The cat – fast asleep on the rug – was keeping warm by the fire. **(1 mark)**

46. Answers will vary. Example: An old lady with white hair asked me for directions to the library. **(1 mark)**

47. were **(1 mark)**

48. My mum, who is a well-known author, has just written a new, action-packed book.
    (1 mark)

49. (which) **(1 mark)**

50. After we left the park, we visited Ash and Paula — the children who live opposite you. **(1 mark)**

Paper 2: Spelling

These are the correct spellings:

1. confidently
2. naughty
3. artificial
4. infectious
5. draught
6. changeable
7. indicating
8. competent
9. competition
10. enough
11. fruit
12. visibly
13. vacancy
14. married
15. chef
16. scissors
17. misspell
18. quickly
19. referee
20. cereal

Set B English reading

James and the Giant Peach

1. Any two from: soft and silver; a million dewdrops; sparkling and twinkling; alive with magic **(1 mark)**

2. That James seems to have no choice but to walk towards the peach. **(1 mark)**

3. gloomy **(1 mark)**

4. Any one from: He didn't act scared because he drank the peach juice as he crawled; He wouldn't have stopped every few seconds to take a bite out of the wall if he was frightened. **(1 mark)**

5. closely **(1 mark)**

6.
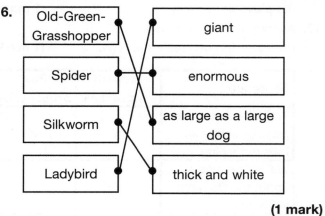

(1 mark)

7. Example: It tells you James is so scared that he wants to run as fast as he can towards the tunnel.

(2 marks for answers that refer to James feeling frightened and wanting to escape quickly; 1 mark for reference to one of these points.)

8. Answers may vary. Examples: The creatures/The Spider, the old-Green-Grasshopper, the Ladybird and the Centipede talk about how hungry they are; the Spider licked her lips; the creatures were all watching him intently. **(2 marks)**

9. Answers may vary. Examples: You have joined us now, you are just the same as us and we will treat you as our friend / family; You are no different from us – we are all here together; He has been enticed into the peach like they have.

(1 mark)

10.

	True	False
A fence surrounded the peach.	✓	
The tunnel was dry and cold.		✓
James bumped his head on the stone in the middle of the peach.	✓	
James couldn't stand up because the peach wasn't big enough.		✓
The creatures were at least the same size as James.	✓	

(1 mark for all five correct)

11. The author is creating suspense. What is going to happen next? Telling us there were four creatures staring, the word 'fixed' creates the image – they were all looking at James, nothing else. The author is helping readers understand the anxiety James must be feeling.

(2 marks: 1 mark for each point made)

12. The Centipede has many feet so has a lot of boots to take off. **(1 mark)**

13. Answers will vary. Examples:
They are going to eat me; I'm so scared; I wish I'd never come here; How on earth am I going to escape? **(3 marks: award 1 mark for each relevant point made)**

About Floella

14. Any one from: It was very different to her life in Trinidad; growing up in two cultures was challenging. **(1 mark)**

15. emigrate **(1 mark)**

16. Floella's mother (Marmie) was a great inspiration to her; her mother gave her lots of love (and encouraged her to do well at school); she often sang with her dad's jazz band.

(3 marks: 1 mark for each)

17. *Within these Walls* **(1 mark)**

18.

Event	Date
Born	1949
Came to England	1960
Made her TV debut	1974
Started her own television production company	1987
Wrote *Coming to England*	1995
Trekked the Great Wall of China	2004

(2 marks: 1 mark if four or five answers are correct, 2 marks if all six answers are correct)

19. in chronological order **(1 mark)**

20. Any one from: Because she was different / from a different country / from a different culture **(1 mark)**

21. Because she had never run at all until she turned 50. **(1 mark)**

22. empathises **(1 mark)**

23. Completed ten London Marathons for Barnardo's; trekked the Great Wall of China for NCH Action for Children; worked and raised money for the NSPCC.

(3 marks: 1 mark for each point)

24.

	Fact	Opinion
She worked in a bank.	✓	
She loved her job on *Play School*.		✓
She presented *Play School* for 12 years.	✓	
She has completed ten London Marathons.	✓	
She is a keen runner.		✓

(1 mark for all correct)

25. Because Floella moved to a new culture when she was a child, she is aware of the difficulties children face in this situation; she wants to help children in a similar position; to help them find their identity; and wants to help them to understand where they came from.

(2 marks: 1 mark for any two points made)

Macavity

26. challenge **(1 mark)**

27. Any one from: Because when they get to crime scene, Macavity is not there; they can't catch Macavity **(1 mark)**

28. The law of gravity is what makes us stay on the ground / stops us floating about in space but Macavity is never there so it is like even gravity can't keep him on the ground.
It is another law that Macavity breaks, as well as every human law.

(2 marks: award 1 mark for each point)

29. appearance **(1 mark)**

30. neglect **(1 mark)**

31. Any one from: Macavity's absence is the main point of the poem; Repetition of the words emphasises Macavity's absence. **(1 mark)**

32.

	Fact	Opinion
It is fun watching Macavity cause trouble.		✓
Macavity's a ginger cat.	✓	
His coat is dusty.	✓	
Macavity has no-one to care for him.		✓

(2 marks for all correct; 1 mark for three correct)

33. He commits crimes / is a thief / is a fiend / is a master criminal because the poet says he can defy the Law.
He is smart / clever because he is never caught by the police / Scotland Yard / the Flying Squad / the Foreign Office / the Admiralty / the Secret Service / can do long division sums.
He is a cheat / deceitful because he cheats at cards.

(3 marks: award 1 mark for each point made with supporting evidence, up to a maximum of 3 marks)

34. Answers will vary. Examples:
Admiration because the writer calls him a 'master criminal', which shows he thinks he is good at what he does. He is able to baffle Scotland Yard, who should be able to catch a mere cat.

(2 marks)

Admiration because the writer says there's no one like Macavity, as if to say there is no one as good as he is. He also says 'there's the wonder of the thing!' which sounds like the writer thinks Macavity's ability to disappear is wonderful.

(2 marks)

Admiration because the writer says that all the other criminal cats are 'nothing more than agents' for Macavity, which means that Macavity is the boss who 'controls their operations'.

(2 marks)

Contempt because the writer says 'he's broken every human law' and he's a 'fiend' and a 'monster'. **(2 marks)**

Contempt because the writer says he is a cat of 'such deceitfulness and suavity'. **(1 mark)**

Set B English grammar, punctuation and spelling

Paper 1: questions

1. mysterious creepy **(1 mark for both correct)**
2. because **(1 mark)**
3. The dog's tail was wagging.
   Six boys' coats were on the floor.

(1 mark for both correct)

4. After the singing, Kenzie blew out the candles.

(1 mark)

5. Mum put the following in my packed lunch: cheese sandwiches, an apple and a yoghurt. **(1 mark)**

6. Grace found a bouncy ball in the garden; she was fairly sure it was Jamal's. **(1 mark)**

7. to find something unacceptable **(1 mark)**

8. Any suitable modal verb, e.g. should; ought (to); could **(1 mark)**

9. celebration **(1 mark)**

10. but **(1 mark)**

11. this letter **(1 mark)**

12. The ice cream van that is in the car park is very popular today. **(1 mark)**

13. The truck drove under the bridge.
    Mum and I strolled along the canal path.

(1 mark for both correct)

14. commas **or** dashes   **(1 mark)**

15. Rosie's homework was too hard for **her** and **she** felt sad that **she** couldn't do it.
                                    (1 mark for all correct)

16. He will go to school tomorrow.   **(1 mark)**

17. What a brilliant book that was   **(1 mark)**

18. Mrs Jones (the Year 5 teacher) played the piano in school today.   **(1 mark)**

19. The flowers that Dad bought for Mum are purple, white and blue.   **(1 mark)**

20. Hanging upside down, the bat made loud noises as the night sky grew darker.   **(1 mark)**

21. Any suitable words, e.g.

Word	Antonym
stiff	bendy
angry	calm

(1 mark for both correct)

22. adverb; noun   **(1 mark for both correct)**

23. Ben has a new puppy called Sid   **(1 mark)**

24. mis   **(1 mark)**

25. I like drawing **and** painting **but / although** my sister prefers writing.
                                    (1 mark for both correct)

26. After tea, we went to the cinema.
                    (1 mark for correct adverbial and correct punctuation)

27. told; spoke; was   **(1 mark for all correct)**

28.

As we were walking to school , we saw Angus who was with his parents.
⌊___S___⌋   ⌊___M___⌋   ⌊___S___⌋

                    (1 mark for all correct)

29. The second sentence means there is more than one singer / shows plural possession.   **(1 mark)**

30. Some hard-working gardeners cut the hedges.
                                    (1 mark)

31.

	Singular	Plural
The <u>children's</u> artwork was displayed in the main corridor.		✓
Our <u>dogs'</u> biggest excitement of the day is the morning walk.		✓
My <u>class's</u> main claim to fame is that we have three sets of twins.	✓	

(1 mark for all correct)

32. My grandfather, always kind and understanding, told me that he would help me with my tricky homework.
          (1 mark for both commas correctly placed)

33. Ella played the piano; Alex played the flute.   **(1 mark)**

34. Moira   **(1 mark)**

35. The walkers are required to wear waterproofs should it rain.   **(1 mark)**

36. Brighton, <u>which is a seaside town</u>, is located on the south coast of England.   **(1 mark)**

37. Answers will vary. Examples:
"Can we have some extra playtime?" the children asked the teacher.
The children asked the teacher, "Can we have some extra playtime?"   **(1 mark)**

38. Liam is determined to win this year's tennis tournament – he's practised day and night.
                                    (1 mark)

39. should've; we'd; wasn't   **(1 mark for all correct)**

40. During his stay on the farm, Jon saw some ducks, a herd of goats and a huge, pink pig.
Accept a colon after 'saw'.   **(1 mark)**

41. (his)   **(1 mark)**

42. I have not got any / I've not got any / I haven't got any.   **(1 mark)**

43. (L)ast (S)aturday, I went to a museum in (E)dinburgh, the capital of (S)cotland, with my uncle.
                    (1 mark for all correct)

44.

Verb	Noun
agree	agreement
assist	assistant / assistance

                    (1 mark for both correct)

45. semi-colon   **(1 mark)**

46. As soon as we reached the cottage, Mum and Dad lit a fire – it was cold even for spring.
                                    (1 mark)

47. is teaching; is intending
                    (1 mark for both correct)

48. kindness; kindly
                    (1 mark for both correct)

49. Annie's mum worked at the school library.
                                    (1 mark)

50. were   **(1 mark)**

Paper 2: Spelling

These are the correct spellings:

1. awkwardly
2. knitting
3. country
4. delicious
5. island
6. favourable
7. promised
8. accommodation
9. potatoes
10. thorough
11. calmly
12. caffeine
13. musician
14. communicating
15. stomach
16. unique
17. cautious
18. vehicle
19. transferred
20. mourning

Spelling test administration

The instructions below are for the spelling tests.

Read the following instruction out to your child:

I am going to read 20 sentences to you. Each sentence has a word missing. Listen carefully to the missing word and fill this in the answer space, making sure that you spell it correctly.

I will read the word, then the word within a sentence, then repeat the word a third time.

You should now read the spellings three times, as given below. Leave at least a 12-second gap between spellings. At the end, read all the sentences again, giving your child the chance to make any changes they wish to their answers.

Set A English grammar, punctuation and spelling

Paper 2: spelling

Spelling 1: The word is **confidently**. The actress performed **confidently** on stage. The word is **confidently**.

Spelling 2: The word is **naughty**. Our **naughty** little kitten had scratched the carpet. The word is **naughty**.

Spelling 3: The word is **artificial**. The flowers in the bathroom are **artificial**. The word is **artificial**.

Spelling 4: The word is **infectious**. The doctor said the rash was highly **infectious**. The word is **infectious**.

Spelling 5: The word is **draught**. There is a **draught** coming from the large window. The word is **draught**.

Spelling 6: The word is **changeable**. The weather is very **changeable** today. The word is **changeable**.

Spelling 7: The word is **indicating**. The car in front was **indicating** right. The word is **indicating**.

Spelling 8: The word is **competent**. James's dad is a very **competent** sailor. The word is **competent**.

Spelling 9: The word is **competition**. Sam won a **competition** he entered at school. The word is **competition**.

Spelling 10: The word is **enough**. I think I have done **enough** homework now. The word is **enough**.

Spelling 11: The word is **fruit**. Mangoes, pineapples, kiwis and oranges are all types of **fruit**. The word is **fruit**.

Spelling 12: The word is **visibly**. Raj was **visibly** shocked to see his old friend again. The word is **visibly**.

Spelling 13: The word is **vacancy**. The hotel sign said there was no **vacancy**. The word is **vacancy**.

Spelling 14: The word is **married**. It is a year since Auntie Jan and Uncle Paddy were **married**. The word is **married**.

Spelling 15: The word is **chef**. The new **chef** has introduced some interesting dishes. The word is **chef**.

Spelling 16: The word is **scissors**. Grace passed the **scissors** carefully to Dan. The word is **scissors**.

Spelling 17: The word is **misspell**. I was very careful not to **misspell** my teacher's name. The word is **misspell**.

Spelling 18: The word is **quickly**. We **quickly** ran for help when we heard the alarm. The word is **quickly**.

Spelling 19: The word is **referee**. Eventually, the **referee** blew the final whistle. The word is **referee**.

Spelling 20: The word is **cereal**. Our family eats **cereal** for breakfast. The word is **cereal**.

Set B English grammar, punctuation and spelling

Paper 2: spelling

Spelling 1: The word is **awkwardly**.
Bea greeted the new member **awkwardly**.
The word is **awkwardly**.

Spelling 2: The word is **knitting**.
Gran likes **knitting** during the long, winter months.
The word is **knitting**.

Spelling 3: The word is **country**.
My ambition is to play football for my **country**.
The word is **country**.

Spelling 4: The word is **delicious**.
The chocolate cake was **delicious**.
The word is **delicious**.

Spelling 5: The word is **island**.
The **island** of Majorca is close to Spain.
The word is **island**.

Spelling 6: The word is **favourable**.
The weather promises to be quite **favourable** this weekend.
The word is **favourable**.

Spelling 7: The word is **promised**.
You **promised** you wouldn't tell.
The word is **promised**.

Spelling 8: The word is **accommodation**.
We do not mind what type of **accommodation** we stay in on holiday.
The word is **accommodation**.

Spelling 9: The word is **potatoes**.
Potatoes can be mashed, chipped, boiled or baked.
The word is **potatoes**.

Spelling 10: The word is **thorough**.
After a **thorough** search, we still couldn't find the keys.
The word is **thorough**.

Spelling 11: The word is **calmly**.
We spoke **calmly** to the hysterical girl.
The word is **calmly**.

Spelling 12: The word is **caffeine**.
Coffee and fizzy drinks usually contain **caffeine**.
The word is **caffeine**.

Spelling 13: The word is **musician**.
A visiting **musician** played his guitar in assembly.
The word is **musician**.

Spelling 14: The word is **communicating**.
Our teacher is good at **communicating** with our parents.
The word is **communicating**.

Spelling 15: The word is **stomach**.
My **stomach** feels full after lunch.
The word is **stomach**.

Spelling 16: The word is **unique**.
Everyone has **unique** fingerprints.
The word is **unique**.

Spelling 17: The word is **cautious**.
We are always **cautious** when we walk down the cliff steps.
The word is **cautious**.

Spelling 18: The word is **vehicle**.
Ned's **vehicle** was the fastest.
The word is **vehicle**.

Spelling 19: The word is **transferred**.
The gymnasts **transferred** their weight across the bars.
The word is **transferred**.

Spelling 20: The word is **mourning**.
The whole family is in **mourning** for our pet.
The word is **mourning**.

**THIS PAGE HAS INTENTIONALLY
BEEN LEFT BLANK**

THIS PAGE HAS INTENTIONALLY
BEEN LEFT BLANK